ACT I
APPETIZERS

Setting the Stage

Produced By

BACKERS VOLUNTEER BOARD OF THE REPERTORY THEATRE OF ST. LOUIS

ACT ONE

Proceeds from *Opening Night Entertaining* will be used to support the cultural and educational activities of The Repertory Theatre of St. Louis.

THE REPERTORY THEATRE OF ST. LOUIS
130 EDGAR ROAD
P.O. BOX 191730
ST. LOUIS, MO 63119

ALL RIGHTS RESERVED
COPYRIGHT PENDING 1993

To order copies of *Opening Night Entertaining*, send a check for $16.95 plus $1.75 for postage and handling to:

Opening Night Entertaining
P.O. Box 8014
St. Louis, MO 63156-8014

(314) 361-4419

DESIGN AND PRODUCTION
Gretchen Floresca
Creative and Design Director
Werremeyer Creative
St. Louis, Mo.

PRINTING
Fleming Printing Company
St. Louis, Mo.

PRINTED ON RECYCLED PAPER

DEDICATION

A truism of the theatre – not less true for being one – is that the stage is a cooperative art form. Unlike a chef in the kitchen who works culinary magic alone, a theatrical production is the work of many – from the stagehands to the actors, who take the bows, to the director, who captains the entire effort.

"COOKERY IS BECOME AN ART,

Yet a theatrical production also needs a theatre. That means the stage is really a communal effort, drawing, as do the volumes you now hold, upon the skills and work of many others besides all the theatrical professionals.

A NOBLE SCIENCE;

And so this dedication: for the few who take the applause; for the many who give it and their time and money; for the volunteers, the members of the Backers Volunteer Board, and everyone in between who has worked for our beloved Rep.

COOKS ARE GENTLEMEN."

This book's for you . . .
and for the theatre you make possible.

ROBERT BURTON

"Sit down and feed, and welcome to our table."

As You Like It
WILLIAM SHAKESPEARE

BACKERS VOLUNTEER BOARD

Ann Augustin	*Dee Laime*	*Trudie Roth*
Sue Barley	*Jean Lange*	*Sue Shapleigh*
Tina Burke	*Patti Lewis*	*Barbara Size*
Carol Chapman	*Jack Lippard*	*Betsy Smith*
Phyllis DeYong	*Barbara Mennell*	*Clare Smith*
Vi Farmer	*Marilyn Monson*	*Gwen Springett*
Mary Franckle	*Harriet Morrison*	*Marion Strachan*
Carol Gast	*Jill Norton*	*Dee Thompson*
Gloria Goetsch	*JoAnne Parrish*	*Linda Vandivort*
Louise Griesbach	*Joyce Patterson*	*William Wiese*
Vivian Kirk	*Brenda Richey*	*Janice Wohlwend*
Judy Kuhlman	*Pat Richter*	*Carolyn Woodruff*

A SOLILOQUY

The houselights fade. The music swells. The stage lights come up on a scene, and that wonderful sense of anticipation fills the air. We all want to know what will happen next. The theatre is full of magic, surprise, and astonishing things. Whetting the appetite for what's to come next on-stage is part of the craft and art of the theatre. The wonderful contributors to this book hope that, by setting your stage, you will be ready to get to the next scene with full anticipation of what could happen next.

Steven Woolf
ARTISTIC DIRECTOR
THE REPERTORY THEATRE OF ST. LOUIS

"The intention of every other piece of praise may be discussed and maybe mistrusted; but the purpose of **A COOKERY BOOK** is one and unmistakable. Its object can conceivably be no other than to increase the happiness of mankind."

Joseph Conrad

APPETIZERS

Contents

BRIE PESTO *10*
ORANGE AND ALMOND BRIE CROSTINI *11*

RISOTTO WITH SPINACH, RADICCHIO, SUN-DRIED TOMATOES,
    AND SMOKED MOZZARELLA *12*
WARM GOAT CHEESE AND ROASTED PECANS *13*

FRESH MUSHROOM PATÉ *14*

TNG'S STUFFED MUSHROOMS *16*
MUSHROOMS IN FILO *17*

BLT POTATOES *18*
EGGPLANT ROLLUPS *19*

RAGOUT OF SPRING ONIONS AND WILD MUSHROOMS IN PUFF PASTRY *20*

LA TERRINE DE LEGUMES, L'AUBERGE'S VEGETABLE TERRINE *22*
ROASTED VEGETABLE TERRINE *23*

HEARTS OF PALM SALAD WITH BALSAMIC MARINADE *24*

ROASTED GARLIC CUSTARD *26*
HUMMUS TAHINI *27*

ACT ONE

Contents

TAPENADE MAYONNAISE *29*

PENNE WITH GORGONZOLA AND SUN-DRIED TOMATOES *30*
CAPELLINI LO RUSSO *31*

SANTA FE RELISH *32*
QUESADILLA LAYER CAKE *33*

PESTO CHICKEN AND RED, YELLOW PEPPERS *34*
CURRIED CHICKEN SALAD *35*

THAI CHICKEN SKEWERS WITH SATAY SAUCE *37*

MARINATED SHRIMP WITH BASIL *38*
RASPBERRY SHRIMP *39*

SHRIMP WONTONS WITH HONEY CHIPOTLE MAYONNAISE *40*

THAI SPICED SHRIMP *42*
SHRIMP POLENTA SQUARES *43*

SHRIMP AND ARTICHOKE BROCHETTE WITH LIME HABEÑERO SAUCE *44*
SHRIMP SCAMPI *45*

RITZ-CARLTON CRAB CAKES WITH LEMON CAPER BEURRE BLANC SAUCE *46*

PICANTE CRAB MOLD *48*
MUSSELS DIJONAISE *49*

APPETIZERS

Contents

ESCARGOT IN FILO *50*

SMOKED OYSTER LOAF *53*

FARFALLE IN SMOKED SALMON CREAM *54*
PEPPER-GRILLED SALMON SERVED ON HORSERADISH CREAM SAUCE *55*

PETITES CRÊPES DE SAUMON FUMÉ EN BOURSE *56*

SMOKED SALMON AND BOURSIN CHEESE ON MINI-BAGELS *58*
SMOKED SALMON QUESADILLAS *59*

SALMON SKEWERS WITH CHINESE MUSTARD GLAZE *60*
SAUTÉED SEA SCALLOPS WITH CHIPOTLE CREAM SAUCE *61*

SCALLOPS AND AVOCADO WITH RED PEPPER COULIS *62*
SCALLOPS CHARDONNAY WITH BASIL AND SHIITAKE MUSHROOMS *63*

SMOKED TROUT MOUSSELINE *65*

MEDALLIONS OF BEEF TENDERLOIN *66*
CARPACCIO *67*

SAUSAGE WELLINGTON *69*

WINES RECOMMENDED BY:

The Cheese Place

The Wine Cellar

West End Wines

ACT ONE

Brie Pesto

SERVES 6

1/4 CUP RICOTTA CHEESE
1/8 CUP PESTO
   (PURCHASED OR HOMEMADE)
1/8 CUP CHOPPED SUN-DRIED TOMATOES
   (DRAINED IF PACKED IN OIL)
1/2 POUND ROUND WHEEL BRIE,
   SLICED HORIZONTALLY
   TO MAKE TWO WHEELS
CLARIFIED BUTTER* (ABOUT 1/2 STICK)
3 (14 x 18 INCH) SHEETS FILO
   DOUGH, THAWED
FRENCH BREAD, THINLY SLICED
VARIETY OF SLICED FRESH FRUIT

* To clarify butter, melt the butter completely over low heat. Remove pan from heat and let it stand a few minutes, allowing the milk solids to settle to the bottom. Skim the butterfat from the top; strain the clear yellow liquid into a container. Discard solids.

*John S. Geers
Webster Grill & Café*

For filling, combine ricotta, pesto, and tomatoes; stir to mix well. Spread filling on bottom half of wheel; replace top half of cheese. Brush melted, clarified butter on each sheet of filo dough as you stack one on top of another. Place Brie on sheets of filo dough. Wrap dough up side of stuffed Brie and fold over top. Butter the outside of the filo. Put Brie, folded side of dough down, onto cookie sheet; bake in a preheated 350-degree oven for 20 to 25 minutes or until done. Brie is done when cheese begins to flow out of the wrapper.

Serve with several serving knives, thinly sliced French bread, and a variety of sliced fresh fruit.

APPETIZERS

Orange and Almond Brie Crostini

SERVES 8

4 OUNCES BRIE

3 TABLESPOONS ORANGE MARMALADE

3 TABLESPOONS ALMOND SLICES, TOASTED

2 TABLESPOONS WHIPPING CREAM

8 SLICES FRENCH BREAD, 1/4-INCH THICK

Combine Brie, marmalade, almonds, and cream in a mixing bowl and beat well. Spread cheese mixture on bread slices. Heat in 350-degree oven for 1 minute or just until cheese melts.

Serve immediately.

Chris Desens
The Country Club
at The Legends

An easy way to enjoy Brie as an hors d'oeuvre

Suggested wine: Riesling or Chenin Blanc

Pygmalion
JOEL FONTAINE
SCENIC DESIGNER

ACT ONE

Risotto with Spinach, Radicchio, Sun-Dried Tomatoes, and Smoked Mozzarella

SERVES 6

1 CARROT
1 RIB OF CELERY
1 YELLOW ONION
OLIVE OIL
1 TEASPOON GARLIC
1/2 POUND BUTTER
2 CUPS RAW SPINACH
1 HEAD RADICCHIO
1/2 CUP SUN-DRIED TOMATOES, BLANCHED
1 POUND ARBORIO RICE
1/2 CUP WHITE WINE
2 CUPS WATER OR CHICKEN STOCK
1 CUP GRATED PARMESAN CHEESE
1/2 CUP SMOKED MOZZARELLA CHEESE
SALT AND FRESHLY GROUND PEPPER TO TASTE

Peel the carrot and rough-chop the celery, carrot, and onion. Mince in a food processor. Set aside. In a large pan, put the oil and garlic and half the butter. Sweat the vegetables until they release their aroma (about 3 minutes). Add the rice and mix thoroughly. When the rice clicks on the sides of the pan (about 5 minutes), add the wine and water or stock. Mix. Continue to cook stirring constantly until thick (approximately 25 to 30 minutes). Add the butter, cheeses, and remaining ingredients.

Zoë Robinson, Owner
Café Zoë

"Oh you must eat your spinach. All little girls should eat their spinach."

WOMAN IN MIND
Alan Ayckbourn

APPETIZERS

Warm Goat Cheese and Roasted Pecans

SERVES 8

1 POUND GOAT CHEESE IN A LOG
3 OUNCES PECAN HALVES
1 SMALL LOAF FRENCH BREAD
OLIVE OIL
ANY COMMERCIAL-TYPE MARINARA SAUCE

*Kathy Schmidt
and Rob Hodes, Chefs
Seven Gables Inn,
Bernard's Bar and Bistro*

Slice goat cheese in 1-inch rounds. Roast pecans in the oven for 1 hour at 100 degrees. Finely chop in food processor. Roll the edges of cheese in the nuts, bake at 350 degrees for about 5 minutes. Slice French bread in 1-inch-thick slices, brush with olive oil, and toast in the oven. Warm marinara sauce in microwave. (When baking goat cheese, it must be baked on the serving platter. You will not be able to slide the cheese onto another dish after it comes out of the oven.) To serve, arrange toasted French bread around goat cheese and serve bowls of warm marinara as a dipping sauce.

Suggested wine: Semillon

ACT ONE

Fresh Mushroom Paté

SERVES 10 TO 12

1/4 CUP BUTTER
1 CUP CHOPPED ONION
1/4 CUP SCALLIONS
3 RIBS CELERY (ABOUT 1 CUP)
4 TEASPOONS MINCED GARLIC
2 POUNDS MUSHROOMS, THINLY SLICED
1/2 CUP WHITE WINE (OPTIONAL)
2 CUPS CHOPPED WALNUTS
(PECANS CAN BE SUBSTITUTED)

1 TABLESPOON DRIED BASIL, CRUMBLED
1 TABLESPOON DRIED THYME, CRUMBLED
1 TABLESPOON DRIED OREGANO, CRUMBLED
1 1/2 TEASPOONS ROSEMARY, CRUMBLED
1 1/2 TEASPOONS SALT
1/2 TEASPOON FRESH CRACKED PEPPER
12 OUNCES CREAM CHEESE, SOFTENED
3/4 CUP FRESH BREAD CRUMBS, DRIED OVERNIGHT AND PROCESSED
3 EGGS, LIGHTLY BEATEN
SPRIG FRESH ROSEMARY (OPTIONAL)
GRAPES (OPTIONAL)
TOAST POINTS OR FRENCH BREAD

Linda Pilcher, Chef
Something Elegant Catering

APPETIZERS

Heat the butter over medium heat. Sauté the onion, scallions, celery, and garlic until soft and golden — about 6 minutes. Increase heat to high and add the mushrooms and white wine. Combine well. Add the walnuts, herbs, salt, and pepper, and cook until the liquid evaporates. Stir in the cream cheese. Remove from the heat and let cool slightly.

"Hors d'oeuvres from our trolley, grapefruit cocktail…"

Put mixture into food processor and process in batches if necessary. Add the bread crumbs and eggs, and puree until smooth or until desired consistency. Pour into greased 9 x 5 x 2 1/2 inch loaf pan (8 to 10 1/2 cup ramekins can be substituted.) Cover with waxed paper and foil. Bake at 350 degrees for 1 1/2 hours (35 to 45 minutes if using ramekins). Cool in the pan. Chill wrapped overnight.

Invert onto a plate.

Confusions-Between Mouthfuls
Alan Ayckbourn

Garnish with sprig of fresh rosemary. Garnish plate with grapes and serve with toast points or sliced French bread.

ACT ONE

TNG's Stuffed Mushrooms

SERVES 5

1 POUND LARGE MUSHROOMS
1 TEASPOON SALT
1 TEASPOON PEPPER
1 TEASPOON GARLIC
1 BUNCH SCALLIONS
1 TEASPOON CAJUN SPICE
1 POUND CREAM CHEESE
1/2 POUND CRAB MEAT
FLOUR
BUTTERMILK
ITALIAN BREADING
PARMESAN CHEESE

Pull core out of mushrooms, wash mushrooms lay out to dry. Combine salt, pepper, garlic, scallions, Cajun spice, cream cheese, and crab meat. Mix gently. With teaspoon, put 1 ounce seafood stuffing in core area. Cover with flour. Dip in buttermilk. Cover with Italian breading (TNG's homemade breading). Fry until golden brown (larger mushrooms take longer). Be careful to fry at 375 degrees with stuffing upright in fryer. Sprinkle fresh Parmesan cheese over mushrooms and serve.

Chris Roseman, Chef
Two Nice Guys

Woman In Mind
JOHN EZELL
SCENIC DESIGNER

APPETIZERS

Mushrooms in Filo

SERVES 8

- 3 TABLESPOONS BUTTER
- 1 CUP SLICED MUSHROOMS
- 1/2 ONION, DICED
- 8 OUNCES CREAM CHEESE
- 1/2 TEASPOON GRANULATED GARLIC
- 4 FILO SHEETS
- 3 TABLESPOONS BUTTER, FOR BRUSHING

Melt butter. Sauté sliced mushrooms and onion in butter until soft. Add cream cheese and garlic to taste. Layer filo by brushing with butter, top with filo and repeat using up to 4 sheets. Spoon mushroom mixture in a row, lengthwise. Roll pastry to make a long roll. Brush with butter. Bake at 400 degrees for 25 minutes.

David Schwartz, Chef
Blayney Catering

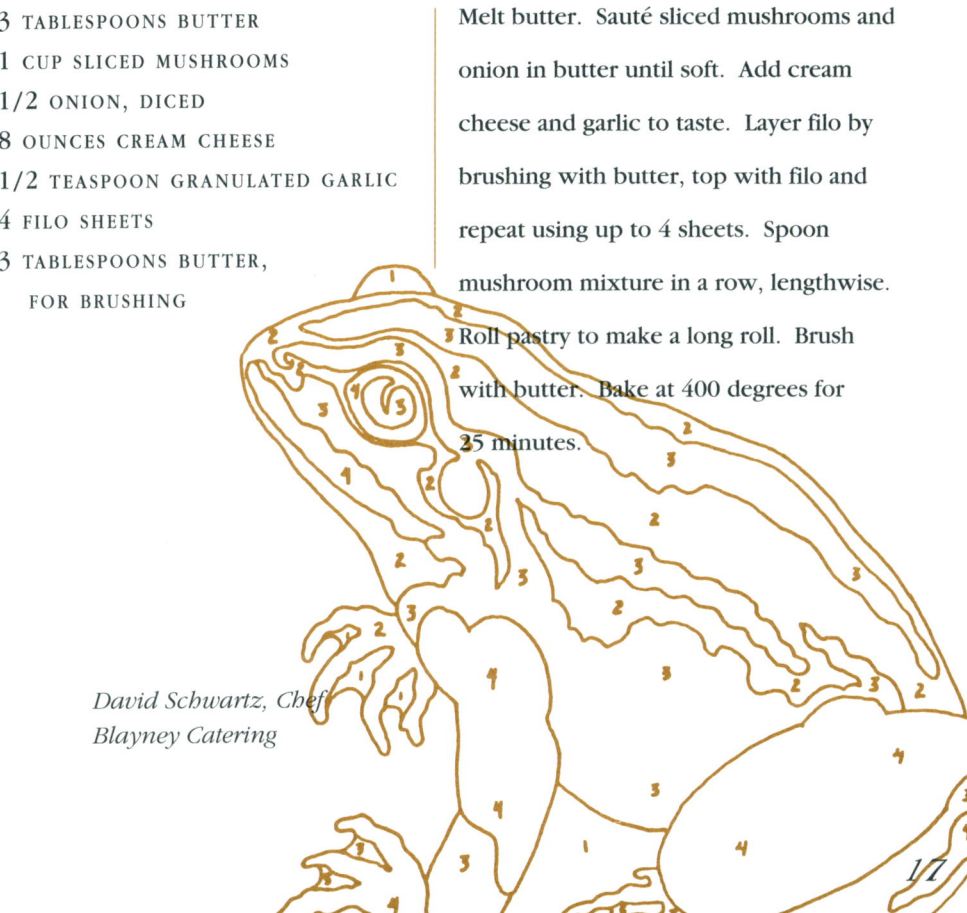

A C T O N E

BLT Potatoes

SERVES 15 TO 18

- 3 POUNDS (OR 36) RED, NEW, BABY POTATOES
- 10 SLICES BACON, COOKED UNTIL CRISP
- 3 TOMATOES, PEELED AND SEEDED
- 1 CUP MAYONNAISE
- 1 TABLESPOON DIJON-STYLE MUSTARD
- 1/4 CUP GREEN ONIONS, MINCED
- 1/4 CUP PARSLEY, MINCED
- DASH OF HOT PEPPER SAUCE

Cook potatoes in boiling water until done. Plunge in cold water to keep from over cooking. Cut off top of potatoes and hollow out potato with melon baller. Set aside. Drain bacon and cool to room temperature. Combine tomatoes, mayonnaise, mustard, onions, parsley, and pepper sauce in food processor, fitted with the metal blade, taking care to preserve the texture. After processing, add crumbled bacon. Stuff potatoes with mixture. Serve cold.

Elizabeth and Mark Dubro
The Backstage Club

Eggplant Rollups

SERVES 8

- 8 1/4-inch thick-sliced eggplant
- 2 tablespoons butter, melted
- 2 ounces cream cheese
- 2 ounces Parmesan cheese
- 2 ounces goat cheese
- 2 ounces provel cheese
- 16 to 25 shrimp, peeled and deveined
- 1 cup spinach, picked
- 1 tablespoon onion, diced
- 1 teaspoon oregano, leaf
- 2 cups tomatoes, thinly sliced
- 1 cup beef stock, thickened
- 1 teaspoon Tabasco Sauce

Mike Wilson, Chef
Big Sky Cafe

Cut off the top of the eggplant, then slice lengthwise. Butter all 8 slices and char-grill until marked with diamond shapes. Let cool. In a bowl combine all of the cheeses and let soften. Sauté the shrimp. When almost cooked, add the spinach and continue sautéing until spinach is wilted. Drain and add to cheese, mix well. Sauté onion, oregano, and tomatoes for about 5 minutes. Add beef stock and Tabasco. Let simmer for 20 minutes. Place eggplant grilled side down. On small end of eggplant, place two shrimp and 2 tablespoons of cheese and spinach mixture. Roll. Heat in oven on oiled pan to keep from sticking. Remove from oven and top with spicy tomato sauce and Parmesan cheese.

ACT ONE

Ragout of Spring Onions and Wild Mushrooms in Puff Pastry

SERVES 4

> "A cucumber should be well-sliced and dressed with pepper and vinegar, and then thrown out, as good for nothing."
>
> — BEN JOHNSON

12 LARGE GREEN ONIONS
4 1-INCH SQUARES PUFF PASTRY DOUGH
1 WHOLE EGG WITH
   1 TEASPOON WATER (EGG WASH)
2 OUNCES UNSALTED BUTTER
12 SMALL SHIITAKE MUSHROOMS, DICED
12 SMALL OYSTER MUSHROOMS, DICED
8 FRESH CÈPES MUSHROOMS
4 TEASPOONS SHALLOTS, FINELY DICED
2 TEASPOONS FRESH HERBS, FINELY CHOPPED
   (SUCH AS THYME, ROSEMARY, PARSLEY)
2 OUNCES WHITE WINE
4 OUNCES VEAL STOCK
4 OUNCES HEAVY WHIPPING CREAM
SALT AND PEPPER TO TASTE
4 FRESH PIECES OF THYME

Brian Stapleton, Executive Chef
The Ritz-Carlton, St. Louis

APPETIZERS

Chop green onions with a sharp chef's knife into 1/8-inch pieces. Save 4 pieces for garnish later. Place 4 squares of puff pastry dough on a nonsticking baking sheet and brush sheets with a small amount of egg wash. Bake in oven at 375 degrees for 7 to 10 minutes until puffed and golden brown. Cook butter and onions in a small sauté pan at medium heat, stirring until slightly softened. Add mushrooms, shallots, and herbs, and continue stirring until mushrooms turn light brown color and release all their water. Deglaze with white wine and add veal stock. Reduce for a few minutes and add cream. Reduce again until the mixture becomes a thick consistency. Remove from heat and season to taste with salt and pepper. Slice puff pastry squares in half and spoon onion mixture on half, placing the other half on top. Garnish each with reserved onion and a fresh piece of thyme.

ACT ONE

La Terrine de Legumes, L'Auberge's Vegetable Terrine

SERVES 12

8 OUNCES CHICKEN, SKINNED AND GROUND
1 EGG WHITE
4 OUNCES 40 PERCENT HEAVY CREAM
1/2 TEASPOON SALT
1/2 TABLESPOON CHOPPED FRESH DILL
1/2 TABLESPOON CHOPPED FRESH BASIL
PINCH WHITE PEPPER
1/2 POUND CARROTS, PEELED AND DICED
4 OUNCES ZUCCHINI, SEEDED AND DICED
4 OUNCES ARTICHOKE BOTTOMS
8 OUNCES GREEN PEAS
4 OUNCES SHIITAKE MUSHROOMS, STEMMED AND CUT IN JULIENNE
8 OUNCES SPINACH, STEMMED
8 OUNCES RED BELL PEPPER
   (4 OUNCES DICED AND
   4 OUNCES JULIENNE)
MAYONNAISE
HERBS

Process chicken and egg white in food processor to a fine paste. Add cream, salt, dill, basil, and white pepper. Steam all vegetables until just tender. Dry vegetables. Fold vegetables into chicken mousse (now it's called a mousseline). Line 12-inch terrine with oil. Layer julienne red pepper and fill mold with mousseline. Cover with foil or a cover. Place terrine in a bain-marie. Fill with hot water. Bake in oven at 350 degrees until internal temperature is 185 degrees. Chill overnight. Serve with mayonnaise and any herb (such as tarragon or dill).

Suggested wine: Beaujolais

Jean-Claude Guillossou, Chef
L'Auberge Bretonne

APPETIZERS

Roasted Vegetable Terrine

SERVES 15

- 1 LEEK
- 3 CARROTS
- 1 EGGPLANT
- 1 ZUCCHINI
- 1 YELLOW SQUASH
- 3 TABLESPOONS FRESH BASIL, CHOPPED
- 1 CUP OLIVE OIL
- 2 YELLOW PEPPERS
- 2 RED PEPPERS
- 1/2 POUND SHIITAKE MUSHROOMS
- 10 OUNCES CHICKEN CONSOMMÉ
- 1/2 OUNCE GELATIN

This is very nice for an outdoor summer gathering and a good accompaniment would be a puree of summer tomatoes.

Jeff Early, Chef
Faust's

Cut off the green end of the leek and reserve. Quarter and wash well the white part of the leek. Cut the carrots, eggplant, and squashes into inch strips. Toss with the basil and olive oil, then bake in the oven on a sheet pan at 200 degrees for about 1 hour. Roast the peppers and shiitake mushrooms together. Skin and seed the peppers. To assemble the terrine, blanch the green part of the leeks and line the terrine. Combine the consommé and gelatin, and warm to a simmer, stirring constantly. Cool and brush the lined terrine with the gelatin mixture (aspic). Layer in vegetables in a colorful manner and ladle about 1 ounce aspic between each layer. When you reach the top, press on the terrine and let the excess aspic spill out of the terrine. Refrigerate overnight and slice to serve.

ACT ONE

Hearts of Palm Salad

SERVES 4

1 1/4 OUNCE CAN HEARTS OF PALM
6 OUNCES BALSAMIC MARINADE
1 LARGE HEAD BIBB LETTUCE
2 OUNCES GORGONZOLA CHEESE
1 TABLESPOON SUN-DRIED TOMATOES

Cut drained hearts of palm at a diagonal and combine with marinade (see page 25) for at least 2 hours. Assemble lettuce leaves on platter and arrange hearts of palm on leaves. Use marinade as the dressing. Garnish with cheese and tomato. Serve with lemon.

Suggested wine: Sauvignon Blanc or Verdicchio

Rich Lo Russo, Chef
Lo Russo's Cucina

APPETIZERS

Balsamic Marinade

MAKES 1 CUP

1/4 CUP BALSAMIC VINEGAR
2 TABLESPOONS RED WINE VINEGAR
2 TABLESPOONS MINCED RED ONION
2 TABLESPOONS PARMESAN CHEESE
1 1/2 TEASPOONS FRESH BASIL
1 1/2 TEASPOONS GRANULATED GARLIC
2 TEASPOONS LEMON JUICE
2 TEASPOONS LIME JUICE
PINCH OF CRACKED BLACK PEPPER
PINCH OF SALT
1/4 CUP EXTRA VIRGIN OIL

Combine all items except oil. Add oil in a slow stream while whisking to cause an emulsion.

Besides the palm salad, this marinade may be used on fish, chicken, or pork. It keeps for weeks in the refrigerator.

The Voyage of The Red Hat
DEVON PAINTER
COSTUME DESIGNER

"The cook who makes no mistakes does not usually make anything."

E.J. Phelps

APPETIZERS

Tapenade Mayonnaise

MAKES 2 TO 3 CUPS

24 TO 30 SOFT, BLACK GREEK OR ITALIAN OLIVES, PITTED
3 TO 4 GARLIC CLOVES
1 1/2 TABLESPOONS CAPERS
1/4 CUP VIRGIN OLIVE OIL
14 TO 16 ANCHOVY FILLETS
4 OUNCES CANNED TUNA FISH
2 TABLESPOONS COGNAC

MAYONNAISE (NOT SALAD DRESSING)
VEGETABLES
TOASTED PITA BREAD
ROMAINE LETTUCE
SHREDDED PARMESAN CHEESE

Scrape and process all in a food processor until it is the consistency of coarse cornmeal. Blend in equal amount of real mayonnaise. Serve with vegetables and toasted pita bread, or toss with Romaine lettuce and shredded Parmesan for a wonderful salad.

Matthew Flatley
Dining In

A Funny Thing Happened on the Way to the Forum
DOROTHY L. MARSHALL
COSTUME DESIGNER

ACT ONE

Santa Fe Relish

3 CUPS

1/2 CUP FROZEN CORN
1/2 CUP BLACK OLIVES, CHOPPED
1/2 CUP RED PEPPERS, DICED
2 TABLESPOONS WHITE ONION, DICED
2 CLOVES GARLIC, MINCED
1/4 TEASPOON PEPPER
1 TEASPOON OREGANO
3 TABLESPOONS OLIVE OIL
1 TABLESPOON LEMON JUICE
1/3 TEASPOON WHITE WINE VINEGAR
SALT
2 RIPE AVOCADOS,
    PEELED AND DICED
TORTILLA CHIPS

*Suggested wine: Beaujolais
or red Zinfandel*

*Sherrill Gonterman
La Chef Catering*

Combine all ingredients except avocado. Add avocado day of party. Everything else should be done the day before. Serve with tortilla chips.

Candide
DOROTHY L. MARSHALL
COSTUME DESIGNER

APPETIZERS

Quesadilla Layer Cake

SERVES 15

- 2 8-OUNCE PACKAGES OF CREAM CHEESE
- 8 OUNCES SOUR CREAM
- 1 SMALL CAN CHOPPED BLACK OLIVES
- 1 SMALL CAN GREEN CHILES
- 4 GREEN ONIONS, CHOPPED
- 1 PACKAGE TACO SEASONING MIX
- 2 PACKAGES LARGE FLOUR TORTILLAS
- 3 CUPS GUACAMOLE
- 1 CUP CHEDDAR CHEESE, GRATED
- 1 CUP TOMATOES, CHOPPED
- 1 CUP GREEN ONIONS, CHOPPED
- 3 CUPS FRESH SALSA

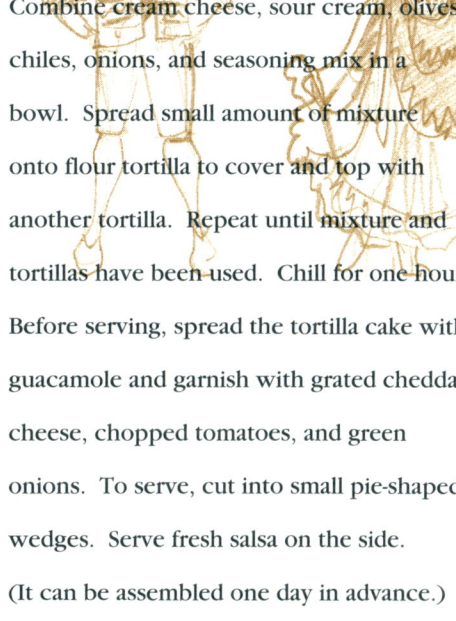

Combine cream cheese, sour cream, olives, chiles, onions, and seasoning mix in a bowl. Spread small amount of mixture onto flour tortilla to cover and top with another tortilla. Repeat until mixture and tortillas have been used. Chill for one hour. Before serving, spread the tortilla cake with guacamole and garnish with grated cheddar cheese, chopped tomatoes, and green onions. To serve, cut into small pie-shaped wedges. Serve fresh salsa on the side. (It can be assembled one day in advance.)

Elizabeth and Mark Dubro
The Backstage Club

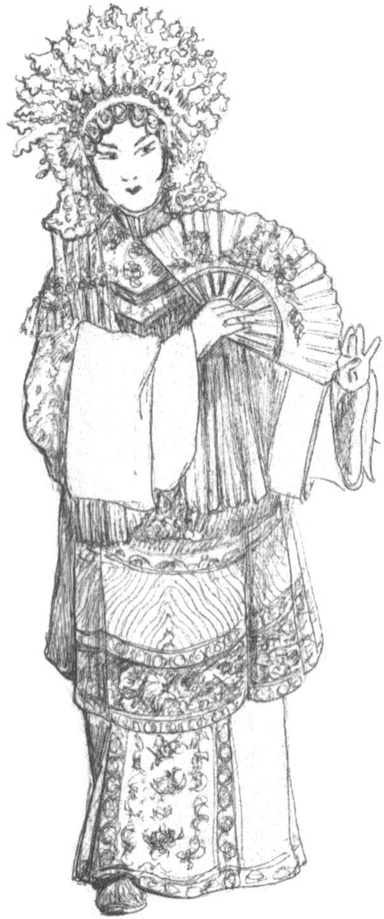

APPETIZERS

Thai Chicken Skewers with Satay Sauce

SERVINGS: 20 SKEWERS

20 BAMBOO SKEWERS SOAKED IN WATER

20 1-OUNCE STRIPS OF CHICKEN BREAST

Marinade for chicken:
2 CLOVES GARLIC, MINCED
2 TABLESPOONS FRESH GINGER, MINCED
4 TABLESPOONS RED ONION, MINCED
8 TABLESPOONS SOY SAUCE
2 TABLESPOONS LIME JUICE
1 TABLESPOON GROUND
  FRESH CHILI PASTE

Satay Sauce:
1 CLOVE GARLIC
2 TABLESPOONS RED ONION
3/4 CUP PEANUT BUTTER
2 TABLESPOONS PEANUT OIL
2 TEASPOONS GROUND
  FRESH CHILI PASTE
2 TEASPOONS SUGAR
1/5 TEASPOON GROUND CORIANDER
8 TABLESPOONS COCONUT MILK

Gregg Mosberger, Chef
Gregory's Creative Cuisine, Inc.

Chicken skewers:

Combine all ingredients for the marinade.

Pour it over chicken and let sit for 1 hour.

Thread chicken strips onto bamboo

skewers and grill until done.

Satay Sauce:

Combine all ingredients except coconut

milk in food processor. With the

processor running slowly, add the

coconut milk until the mixture becomes

smooth. Serve at room temperature.

Suggested wines: Sancerre,
  Pouilly Fumé
  or Gewürztraminer

M. Butterfly
MARIE ANNE CHIMENT
COSTUME DESIGNER

ACT ONE

Marinated Shrimp with Basil

SERVES 4

1 RIPE AVOCADO
3 OUNCES OLIVE OIL
1 OUNCE BALSAMIC VINEGAR
1 TEASPOON POMMEREY OR
   DIJON MUSTARD
CRACKED PEPPER AND SALT TO TASTE
3 LEAVES FRESH BASIL
20 LARGE SHRIMP (SIZE 10/15)

Peel and dice ripe avocado and set aside. To make vinaigrette, mix olive oil, balsamic vinegar, mustard, pepper, salt, and basil. Marinate shrimp in vinaigrette for 4 hours. Charbroil shrimp for 2 minutes on each side. Chill shrimp. Toss with remaining vinaigrette and diced avocado. Serve cold.

Suggested wine:
Sauvignon Blanc

Jean-Claude Guillossou, Chef
L'Auberge Bretonne

APPETIZERS

Raspberry Shrimp

SERVES 4 TO 6

Marinade:
- 1/4 CUP SOY SAUCE
- 1/3 CUP SESAME OIL
- 2 CLOVES GARLIC, MINCED
- 1 TEASPOON GINGER
- 2 TABLESPOONS DIJON MUSTARD

- 2 DOZEN MEDIUM SHRIMP, PEELED AND DEVEINED
- 1 JAR POLANER SEEDLESS RASPBERRY JELLY
- 1 SHOT OF CHAMBORD LIQUEUR

Marinate shrimp for one day. Grill shrimp until done or broil in oven, watching closely so they do not burn. Meanwhile, warm jelly over the stove or in a microwave until jelly becomes loose. Add the Chambord and mix well. When the shrimp are done, skewer with a long toothpick and dip shrimp in jelly mixture to coat.

Suggested wine: Vouvray

*Kathy Schmidt
and Rob Hodes, Chefs
Seven Gables Inn,
Bernard's Bar and Bistro*

ACT ONE

Shrimp Wontons with Honey Chipotle Mayonnaise

SERVINGS: 20 WONTONS

Shrimp Wontons:

1 BUNCH GREEN ONIONS
1 SMALL RED ONION
1/2 CUP CLAM JUICE
20 WONTON WRAPPERS
2 WHOLE EGGS, WHIPPED
20 FRESH BASIL LEAVES
20 MEDIUM SHRIMP, PEELED
  AND DEVEINED

Honey Chipotle Mayonnaise:

1 CUP HEAVY MAYONNAISE
3 TABLESPOONS HONEY
1 TABLESPOON BARBEQUE SAUCE
2 WHOLE CHIPOTLES
  (CANNED IN ADOBO SAUCE)
1 TABLESPOON CILANTRO
2 TABLESPOONS SCALLIONS

Gregg Mosberger, Chef
Gregory's Creative Cuisine, Inc.

APPETIZERS

Shrimp Wontons:

Rough-chop scallions and red onion, and combine with clam juice over medium heat. Cook until clam juice is almost gone. Remove from heat and cool. In food processor, pulse onion mixture until almost smooth. Lay out a wonton wrapper and brush with egg wash. In center of wonton, place the following in order: 1 basil leaf, 1 whole shrimp and 1/2 teaspoon of the onion mixture. Fold the wonton over, corner to corner. Then fold the two base corners in, until they touch; pinch to secure. Fry at 325 degrees until golden brown.

Honey Chipotle Mayonnaise:

Combine all ingredients in food processor and pulse until smooth. Cover and refrigerate until needed.

Suggested wines: Beaujolais, Pinot Noir or Riesling

M. Butterfly
MARIE ANNE CHIMENT
SCENIC DESIGNER

ACT ONE

Thai Spiced Shrimp

SERVES 4

1/4 CUP TERIYAKI SAUCE
1/8 CUP SOY SAUCE
1/8 CUP HOISIN SAUCE
1 TABLESPOON OYSTER SAUCE
1/2 CUP CHICKEN STOCK
1 TABLESPOON GINGER, CHOPPED
2 TABLESPOONS FRESH LEMON GRASS
1/2 TEASPOON CILANTRO, CHOPPED
1 JALAPEÑO PEPPER,
   DICED WITHOUT SEEDS
12 JUMBO SHRIMP
2 TABLESPOONS PEANUT OIL

Combine teriyaki, soy, hoisin, and oyster sauces in a saucepan. Add chicken stock, ginger, lemon grass, cilantro, and jalapeño pepper, and mix with a whisk. Cook over low heat for 10 minutes and adjust seasonings as desired. Pour mixture through a strainer. Sauté shrimp in peanut oil over medium-high heat in a skillet until lightly browned. Garnish shrimp with sauce and serve.

Terrence Hamner, Chef
The Grill
The Ritz-Carlton, St. Louis

Rain. Some Fish. No Elephants.
JOHN CARVER SULLIVAN
COSTUME DESIGNER

APPETIZERS

Shrimp Polenta Squares

SERVES 8

1 OUNCE SUN-DRIED TOMATOES IN OIL
1 CUP CHICKEN BROTH
1/2 CUP YELLOW CORNMEAL
1/4 CUP SLICED GREEN ONION
1/4 TEASPOON SALT
1/8 TEASPOON PEPPER
2 EGGS, SLIGHTLY BEATEN
1 TABLESPOON CILANTRO, SNIPPED
16 FRESH MEDIUM SHRIMP, PEELED

Drain and finely chop tomatoes (should have 2 tablespoons). Line an 8 x 8 x 2 inch baking pan with foil; grease foil. In a saucepan bring broth to a boil. Add cornmeal slowly, stirring constantly. Add tomatoes, onion, 1/4 teaspoon salt and 1/8 teaspoon pepper. Simmer 4 or 5 minutes or until very thick. Remove from heat; let stand 5 minutes. Stir in eggs and cilantro. Spread into prepared pan. Arrange shrimp on top; press lightly. Bake in 400-degree oven for 10 minutes. Let stand 5 minutes. Cut into squares.

David Schwartz, Chef
Blayney Catering

ACT ONE

Shrimp and Artichoke Brochette with Lime Habeñero Sauce

SERVES 12

Skewers:

24 WOODEN SKEWERS,
   SOAKED IN WARM WATER
48 QUARTERED ARTICHOKE HEARTS
48 16/20 SHRIMP

Sauce:

1 CUP WHITE WINE
3 CUPS CHICKEN STOCK
1 STICK BUTTER
3 LIMES (JUICE)
1/2 HABEÑERO PEPPER, MINCED
SALT AND PEPPER TO TASTE

Skewers:

Soak skewers at least 15 minutes. It will prevent them from splintering. Skewer one artichoke then shrimp; repeat until skewer is full. When finished, grill skewers. Serve two skewers per person. Ladle sauce over shrimp and artichokes.

Sauce:

Reduce white wine by half. Add all other ingredients. Bring to a boil. Thicken by using corn starch and cold water. Thicken enough to coat a spoon.

Lisa Slay, Chef
Blue Water Grill

APPETIZERS

Shrimp Scampi

SERVES 4

1/2 CUP BUTTER, UNSALTED, SOFTENED
1 TABLESPOON GARLIC POWDER
1/2 TEASPOON PAPRIKA
1/4 TEASPOON BLACK PEPPER
1 TEASPOON A-1 STEAK SAUCE
1 TEASPOON WORCESTERSHIRE SAUCE
1/4 TEASPOON SALT
1/4 TEASPOON THYME, DRIED
2 TABLESPOONS VEGETABLE OIL
20 SHRIMP, SIZE 10/15 PREFERRED, PEELED AND DEVEINED
4 TO 8 SOUR DOUGH BREAD SLICES (DEPENDING ON SIZE)
LEMON, CUT INTO WEDGES FOR GARNISH

Whip butter on low in a medium mixing bowl. Add next 7 ingredients slowly until well mixed. Increase speed to high and whip butter until fluffy. Set aside. Heat skillet until very hot (almost smoking), carefully add vegetable oil, add shrimp and sauté approximately 3 to 4 minutes or just until the shrimp turn pink. Set aside. Toast both sides of sour dough bread and set aside. In an oven-proof serving dish (large enough to hold the shrimp in one layer), spread half of the whipped butter mixture. Arrange the partially cooked shrimp over the butter and place under the broiler for approximately 1 minute or until butter is bubbling hot. Serve with toast and garnish with lemon wedges.

Pat Cleary, Chef
Bristol Bar and Grill

ACT ONE

Ritz-Carlton Crab Cakes

SERVES 6

1 DICED GREEN PEPPER, SKIN, SEEDS AND MEMBRANE REMOVED
1 DICED RED PEPPER, SKIN, SEEDS AND MEMBRANE REMOVED
3 TABLESPOONS CLARIFIED BUTTER
3 TABLESPOONS FLOUR
1 CUP WHITE WINE
2 TABLESPOONS PREPARED MUSTARD
PEPPER AND SALT TO TASTE
2 POUNDS JUMBO CRAB MEAT OR FLAKED CRAB MEAT

Sauté diced green pepper and red pepper in clarified butter until heated through but still firm. Add flour and white wine, and cook until thick. Remove from the heat and add mustard, ground pepper, salt, and crab meat. Shape into cakes. Sauté in butter until brown.

Serve with Lemon Caper Beurre Blanc Sauce (see page 47).

Terrence Hamner, Chef
The Grill
The Ritz-Carlton, St. Louis

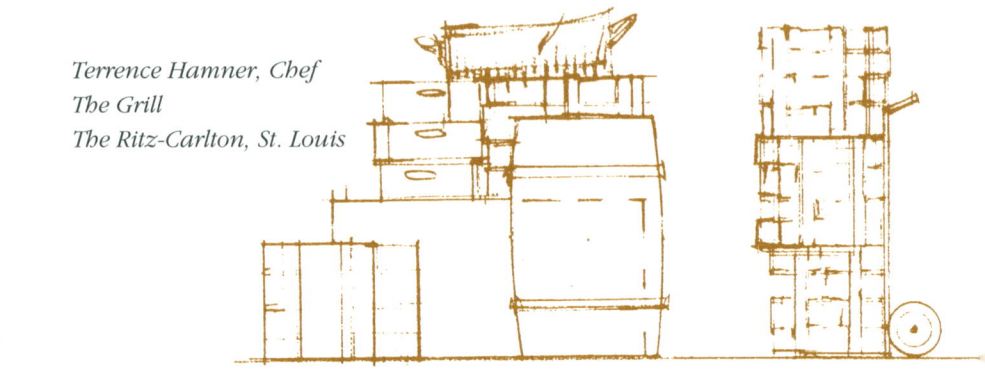

APPETIZERS

Lemon Caper Beurre Blanc Sauce

1 SMALL, FINELY CHOPPED SHALLOT
1 TEASPOON OLIVE OIL
1 CUP DRY WHITE WINE
2 TEASPOONS VINEGAR
1/2 CUP CREAM
1/2 POUND BUTTER, UNSALTED, SOFTENED
1/2 TABLESPOON LEMON JUICE
1 TABLESPOON CAPERS, CHOPPED

Sauté chopped shallot in olive oil until glossy. Add dry white wine and vinegar; simmer and reduce to half its original volume. Reduce heat and add cream. Heat until slowly simmering, and whisk in unsalted butter, a little at a time, beating constantly with a sauce whisk until the sauce is creamy and whitened. Do not boil. Stir in lemon juice and chopped capers, and serve immediately.

Pygmalion
JOEL FONTAINE
SCENIC DESIGNER

Picante Crab Mold

SERVES 8 TO 10

- 1 ENVELOPE UNFLAVORED GELATIN
- 1/4 CUP WATER
- 1 CUP PICANTE SALSA
- 8 OUNCES CREAM CHEESE
- 1/4 CUP CHOPPED ONION
- 1/2 CUP CHOPPED CELERY
- 2 TABLESPOONS CHOPPED GREEN PEPPER
- 2 DASHES OF HOT PEPPER SAUCE
- 2 6-OUNCE CANS CRAB MEAT
- 1 CUP SALAD DRESSING (SUCH AS MIRACLE WHIP)
- WATER CRACKERS OR TORTILLA CHIPS

Dissolve gelatin in water. Heat salsa to a boil. Add gelatin and stir well. Add cream cheese and whisk until smooth. Cool. Add onion, celery, pepper, hot pepper sauce, and crab. Fold in salad dressing. Pour into a lightly oiled mold and chill until firm. Serve with water crackers or tortilla chips.

David Schwartz, Chef
Blayney Catering

Mussels Dijonaise

SERVES 4, 6 MUSSELS EACH

1 TABLESPOON VEGETABLE OIL
24 MUSSELS
1 CUP WHITE WINE
1 MEDIUM SHALLOT, MINCED
1/2 CLOVE GARLIC, MINCED
1 TABLESPOON DIJON-STYLE MUSTARD
1/2 TABLESPOON SOY SAUCE
1 TABLESPOON FRESH LEMON JUICE
SALT AND FRESH GROUND PEPPER
   TO TASTE
1/4 CUP OLIVE OIL

*Suggested wine: Chardonnay
or Pinot Noir*

*Fio Antognini
Fio's Restaurant*

In a large stock pot, heat the vegetable oil until it begins to smoke. Add the mussels and wine, cover and cook over moderate heat, shaking the pot occasionally until the mussels open, 5 to 7 minutes. Remove the mussels with a slotted spoon; let cool and set aside. Discard the cooking liquid and any mussels that have not opened. In a small bowl, combine the shallots, garlic, mustard, soy sauce, lemon juice, salt and pepper. Gradually whisk in the olive oil in a slow, steady stream. Arrange the mussels on the half shell and spoon some of the sauce over each. Chill and enjoy.

ACT ONE

Escargot in Filo

SERVES 4

You can serve this with a simple sauce made from 1 tablespoon shallots, 1 tablespoon garlic, sweated in 1 tablespoon butter then flamed with some Pernod. After this has nearly evaporated, add 1 cup of cream and reduce by half. Add some fresh, chopped basil and salt and pepper to taste. Cook another 3 minutes. Spoon some of the sauce in the center of the plate and place a filo bag on top.

8 TABLESPOONS BUTTER
24 SNAILS
6 SHIITAKE MUSHROOMS
1 CLOVE GARLIC, MINCED
1 SHALLOT, MINCED
1 OUNCE PERNOD
SALT AND FRESHLY GROUND PEPPER
24 5 x 5 INCH FILO SHEETS
MELTED BUTTER FOR BRUSHING

"STRANGE TO SEE HOW A GOOD DINNER AND FEASTING RECONCILE EVERYONE."

SAMUEL PEPYS

Jeff Early, Chef
Faust's

APPETIZERS

Slowly melt a stick of butter in a large skillet. Add the snails, mushrooms, garlic, and shallot. Cook this for about 5 minutes and flame with the Pernod. Put in the refrigerator to cool completely. Lay out the filo sheets and cover them with a damp paper towel. Take 1 sheet at a time and brush it with the melted butter. Repeat this until you have 6 layers. Bunch 6 snails in the center of the filo. Place some of the solidified butter on top of the snails. Bring up the corners of the filo and pinch them together forming a little bag or purse. Repeat this process with all the bags. Brush them with butter and bake them in a 350-degree oven for about 10 minutes or until they are nicely browned. Serve immediately.

*Suggested wine: Pinot Grigo
or Vinho Verde*

"You're as eloquent as an oyster."

The Glass Menagerie
TENNESSEE WILLIAMS

Henry IV, Part I
ALAN ARMSTRONG
COSTUME DESIGNER

APPETIZERS

Smoked Oyster Loaf

SERVES 4

8 OUNCES CREAM CHEESE, SOFTENED
1 TEASPOON WORCESTERSHIRE SAUCE
DASH OF ONION SALT
1 1/2 TABLESPOONS MAYONNAISE
3 OUNCES SMOKED OYSTERS,
    DRAINED AND CHOPPED
3 TABLESPOONS GREEN ONIONS, MINCED
GOURMET CRACKERS

Combine cream cheese, Worcestershire, onion salt, and mayonnaise. Blend well. Spread 1/2 inch thick on a waxed paper-lined jelly roll pan. Chill 30 minutes. Spread oysters on cheese mixture. Roll like a jelly roll. Sprinkle chopped onions on top. Serve with gourmet crackers.

David Schwartz, Chef
Blayney Catering

Suggested wine: Chardonnay

ACT ONE

Farfalle in Smoked Salmon Cream

SERVES 4 TO 6

- 2 CUPS HEAVY CREAM
- 2 CUPS HALF-AND-HALF
- 1 TEASPOON MINCED GARLIC
- 1 BAY LEAF
- 10 WHOLE BLACK PEPPERCORNS
- 2 FLUID OUNCES GOOD BRANDY OR SHERRY
- 1 TEASPOON GRANULATED SUGAR
- 1 DICED SHALLOT
- SALT AND WHITE PEPPER TO TASTE
- 5 OUNCES SMOKED SALMON
- 2 TEASPOONS CORNSTARCH
- 8 OUNCES FARFALLE (BOW TIES), COOKED AND DRAINED

Place all ingredients except cornstarch and farfalle pasta over medium heat. Stir frequently. Bring just to a boil, reduce heat and simmer for 30 minutes. Strain into another pot and whisk in cornstarch mixed with water. Simmer 10 minutes. Toss with cooked farfalle pasta.

Garnish with green peas and as good a caviar as the occasion warrants.

James Nardulli, Chef
Patty Long's 9th Street Abbey

Pepper-Grilled Salmon Served on Horseradish Cream Sauce

SERVES 4

- 4 1-OUNCE SALMON CUTS
- 2 TABLESPOONS GARLIC OIL
- 4 TABLESPOONS 1/4 CRACKED BLACK PEPPER

Horseradish Cream Sauce:
- 1 CUP WHIPPING CREAM
- 3 OUNCES GRATED HORSERADISH ROOT
- 1 LEMON, SQUEEZED
- 1 TEASPOON SALT
- 1 TEASPOON PEPPER
- 1 TEASPOON GARLIC, MINCED

Coat salmon with garlic oil and toss in 1/4 cracked pepper. Grill salmon until diamond stripes appear on both sides (about 1 minute per side). Serve over horseradish cream sauce.

Horseradish Cream Sauce:

In pan, combine whipping cream, horseradish root, lemon juice, salt, pepper, and garlic. Simmer until the back of the spoon is coated. Note: keep heat on low so cream does not scorch.

Mike Wilson, Chef
Big Sky Cafe

A C T   O N E

Petites Crêpes de Saumon Fumé en Bourse

SERVES 24

Crêpes:

5 OUNCES FLOUR

3 EGGS

1/4 TEASPOON SALT

1/8 TEASPOON PEPPER

1/8 TEASPOON NUTMEG

1 1/2 CUPS MILK

1 TABLESPOON CHIVES

2 TABLESPOONS OIL

Mix well and set aside for 1 hour. Use a 5-inch crêpe pan to make nice, small, thin crêpes.

Sauce Ingredients:

5 TABLESPOONS SOUR CREAM

1 TABLESPOON CAPERS

1 TEASPOON CAPER VINEGAR

1 TEASPOON BALSAMIC VINEGAR

Filling:

1 1/2 POUNDS SMOKED SALMON, DICED (USE A GOOD SCOTCH OR IRISH SALMON)

2 HARD BOILED EGGS, DICED

4 TABLESPOONS CAPERS, DRAINED (RESERVE LIQUID)

2 TABLESPOONS CHIVES, FINELY CHOPPED

SALT AND PEPPER TO TASTE

Suggested wine: Pinot Gris Trimbach, Fumé Blanc, or Meursault

Jean Pierre Auge, Chef
Mark Twain Bancshares, Inc.

Pygmalion
JOEL FONTAINE
SCENIC DESIGNER

A P P E T I Z E R S

Place the filling ingredients in a mixing bowl and add half of the sauce. Stir and add more sauce if needed to make a good mixture, but not runny. Halve 20 long pieces of chives, lightly blanched. Place each crêpe flat on table, place a tablespoon of salmon mixture in the center and bring each side of the crêpe together and flute like a purse. Tie with a piece of chive and set on plate or tray. Cover with Saran Wrap and put in refrigerator.

To serve: Spoon one tablespoon of sauce in the center of plate, place purse in the center and decorate with 2 slices of lemon and julienne chives.

ACT ONE

Smoked Salmon and Boursin Cheese on Mini-Bagels

SERVES 4

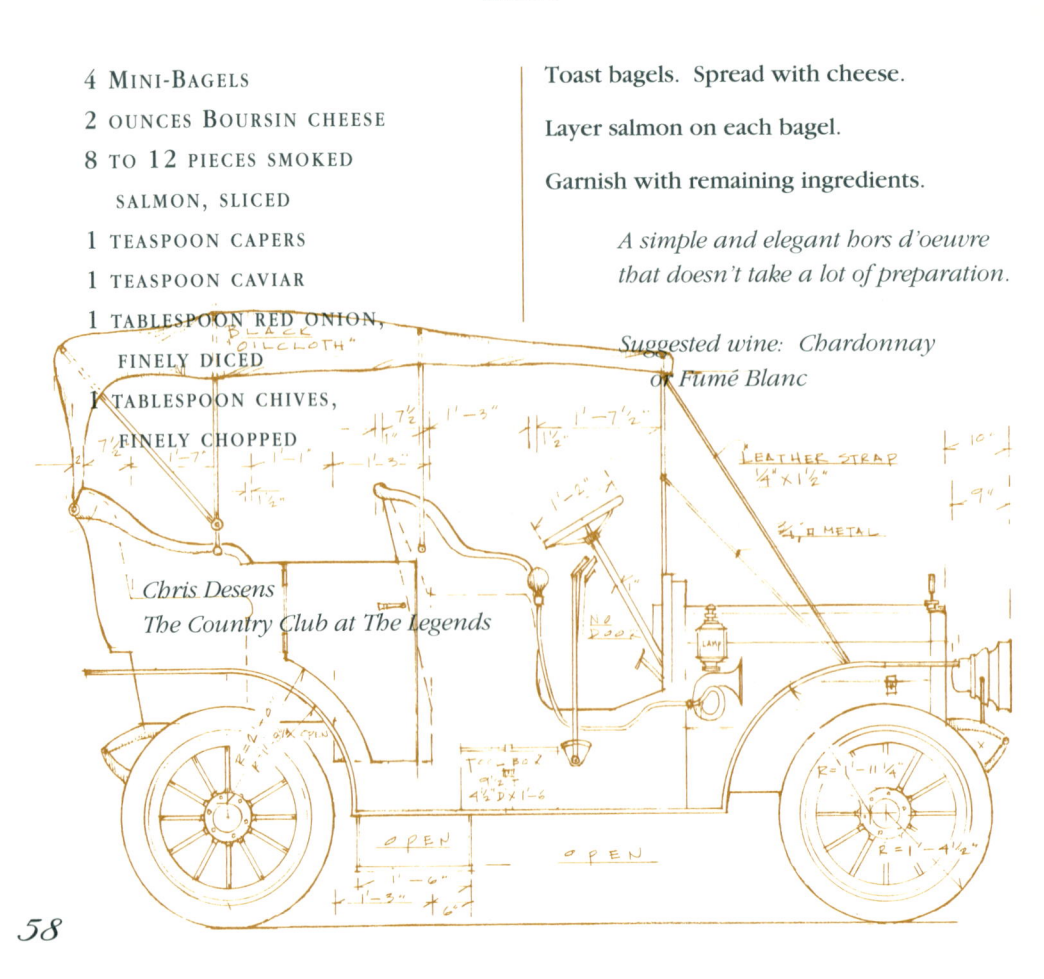

- 4 MINI-BAGELS
- 2 OUNCES BOURSIN CHEESE
- 8 TO 12 PIECES SMOKED SALMON, SLICED
- 1 TEASPOON CAPERS
- 1 TEASPOON CAVIAR
- 1 TABLESPOON RED ONION, FINELY DICED
- 1 TABLESPOON CHIVES, FINELY CHOPPED

Toast bagels. Spread with cheese.

Layer salmon on each bagel.

Garnish with remaining ingredients.

A simple and elegant hors d'oeuvre that doesn't take a lot of preparation.

Suggested wine: Chardonnay or Fumé Blanc

Chris Desens
The Country Club at The Legends

APPETIZERS

Smoked Salmon Quesadillas

SERVES 6

4 OUNCES CREAM CHEESE, SOFTENED
6 FLOUR TORTILLA SHELLS
1 TOMATO, THINLY SLICED
1/2 POUND SMOKED SALMON
3 OUNCES CHEDDAR CHEESE
SALSA
SOUR CREAM
FRESH CHIVES

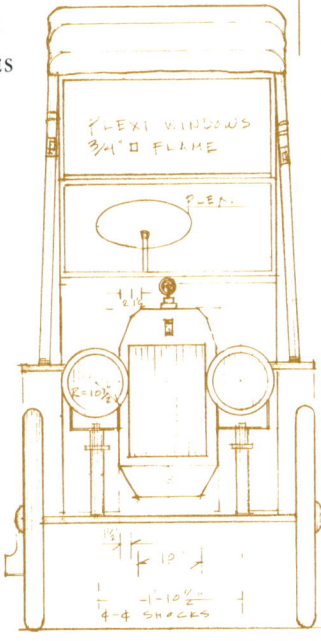

Spread softened cream cheese on half of each tortilla, layer with sliced tomatoes, smoked salmon, and cheddar cheese. Fold in half. Bake in a 350-degree oven for 5 minutes or until brown, or pan fry in skillet until brown on both sides. Cut in wedges and serve with salsa and sour cream, with fresh chives.

Suggested wine: Chardonnay

Kathy Schmidt and Rob Hodes, Chefs
Seven Gables Inn,
Bernard's Bar and Bistro

Pygmalion
JOEL FONTAINE
SCENIC DESIGNER

ACT ONE

Salmon Skewers with Chinese Mustard Glaze

MAKES 20 SKEWERS

Chinese Mustard Glaze:
1/2 CUP GROUND MUSTARD
1/2 CUP SUGAR
1/4 CUP WATER
1/2 CUP HONEY
1/4 CUP SOY SAUCE
1 TEASPOON GROUND BLACK PEPPER

20 1-OUNCE STRIPS OF SALMON
20 BAMBOO SKEWERS, SOAKED
   IN WATER

Combine all ingredients for mustard glaze in a sauce pan and bring to a slow boil. Stir constantly until sugar is dissolved. Remove from heat and refrigerate until cool. Marinate salmon strips in glaze for 45 minutes. Remove salmon from marinade and thread onto bamboo skewers. Grill until just done. Do not overcook.

Suggested wine: Chardonnay

Gregg Mosberger, Chef
Gregory's Creative Cuisine, Inc.

Sautéed Sea Scallops with Chipotle Cream Sauce

SERVES 12

Sauce:

1 CUP WHITE WINE
2 CUPS CHICKEN STOCK
2 CUPS WHIPPING CREAM
2 TABLESPOONS CHIPOTLE PEPPERS, PUREED
1 TABLESPOON CHOPPED GARLIC
SALT AND PEPPER TO TASTE
CORNSTARCH
COLD WATER

MARGARINE
3 POUNDS SEA SCALLOPS
1 BAG SPINACH

Reduce white wine by half. Add the chicken stock, whipping cream, peppers, garlic, salt, and pepper. Bring to a boil and thicken with cornstarch and cold water. Sauce can be made ahead of time and will keep for 4 to 5 days.

Sauté scallops using a large skillet with enough margarine to barely cover the bottom. Add cream sauce to the skillet to help cook the scallops. When scallops are done, spoon over spinach. If you prefer to cook the spinach, also add it to the sauce and scallops. Leaving the spinach leafy adds a nice texture, and the sauce, when poured over, practically cooks it.

Lisa Slay, Chef
Blue Water Grill

Scallops and Avocado with Red Pepper Coulis

SERVES 8

3 POUNDS SEA SCALLOPS
1/2 CUP WATER
1 CUP WHITE WINE
1 CUP LEMON JUICE
SALT AND PEPPER TO TASTE
1/2 TEASPOON PAPRIKA

Sauce:
3 RED PEPPERS
1/2 TEASPOON SALT
CAYENNE TO TASTE
1 1/2 CUPS OLIVE OIL
1 1/2 CUPS CREAM
2 AVOCADOS, RIPE, QUARTERED
PARSLEY

Suggested wine: Chardonnay

Rinse and clean muscle off scallops. Poach scallops in water and white wine for one minute. Marinate overnight in lemon juice, salt and pepper, and paprika. Broil red peppers till charred. Put them in paper bag and keep it closed for 10 minutes. Peel off skin and remove seeds. Puree peppers, add salt and cayenne. Drizzle in oil. Stir in cream and chill. Peel quartered avocados, dip in lemon juice. Puddle red pepper sauce on plate, add avocado quarters, sprinkle with chilled scallops. Garnish with parsley.

Sherrill Gonterman
La Chef Catering

APPETIZERS

Scallops Chardonnay with Basil and Shiitake Mushrooms

SERVES 4

- 1 POUND BAY SCALLOPS
- 1 CUP HEAVY CREAM
- 1/3 CUP CHARDONNAY
- 1 TABLESPOON FRESH BASIL
- 2 TABLESPOONS MELTED BUTTER
- 2 TABLESPOONS SIFTED FLOUR
- 8 OUNCES SHIITAKE MUSHROOMS, CUT IN HALF
- SALT TO TASTE
- 4 READY-TO-SERVE PUFF PASTRY SHELLS

Suggested wine: white Burgundy

*Jean-Claude Guillossou, Chef
L'Auberge Bretonne*

Rinse and drain the scallops and set aside. Place the cream, Chardonnay, fresh basil in a double boiler and set aside. Make a roux by mixing the butter and flour, and heat in a sauté pan until the mixture becomes a light golden color. Slowly add the roux to the double boiler mixture, stirring until it begins to thicken over medium heat. Add the scallops and mushrooms to sauce. Season to desired taste. The scallops and mushrooms cook in the heated sauce without more heat being added. They should be a little underdone in the center. Pour the scallops into the heated puff pastry shells and serve. This also can be served over any pasta dish.

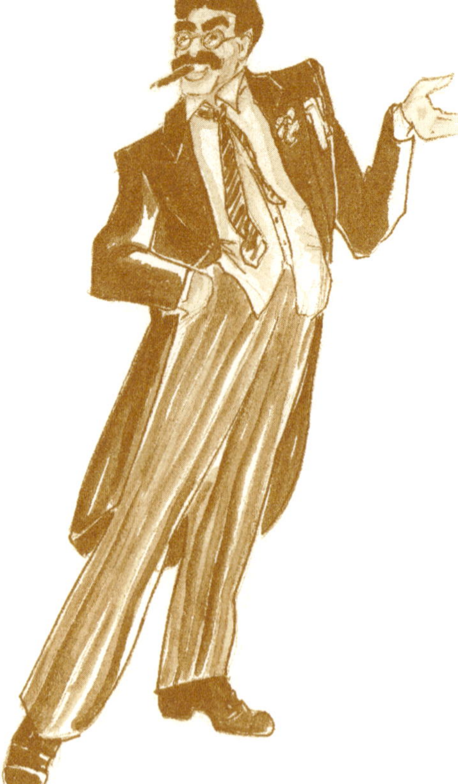

APPETIZERS

Smoked Trout Mousseline

SERVES 8 TO 10

2 SMOKED TROUT FILLETS
1/4 POUND BUTTER,
  ROOM TEMPERATURE
1/2 CUP HEAVY CREAM
JUICE OF 1 LEMON
TABASCO SAUCE TO TASTE

1/2 CUP SOUR CREAM
4 OUNCES RED SALMON CAVIAR
DILL SPRIGS
LEMON SLICES
WATER BISCUITS

Matthew Flatley
Dining In

Skin trout fillets, break into pieces and let them come to room temperature. Place trout and butter in processor and pulse several times scraping down sides of bowl. Add cream, lemon juice, and Tabasco, and process until very smooth. Place in an 8-inch round cake pan that is lined with Saran Wrap and press and mold into pan firmly. Let cool several hours or overnight. Invert the mousseline onto a serving platter. Spread sour cream on top. Spoon caviar over entire surface. Decorate and garnish with the dill and lemon. Serve with biscuits.

A Day In Hollywood
  A Night In The Ukraine
DOROTHY L. MARSHALL
COSTUME DESIGNER

ACT ONE

Medallions of Beef Tenderloin

SERVES 8

1 POUND MUSHROOMS, SLICED (SHIITAKE, OYSTER, PORTEBELLO, CREMINI)
2 TABLESPOONS OLIVE OIL
2 OUNCES DRY WHITE WINE
16 OUNCES CONCENTRATED BEEF STOCK
SALT AND PEPPER
1 POUND TRIMMED BEEF TENDERLOIN
FRESH TARRAGON
BAGUETTE ROUNDS

In a large skillet over high heat, sauté mushrooms in olive oil. When they start to become soft, deglaze with white wine. Add stock, salt and pepper, and reduce to desired texture. Set aside. Grill tenderloin. Slice and top with sauce. Garnish with tarragon. Serve on baguette rounds.

David Timmey
Balaban's

Suggested wine: Merlot

"Doth not the appetite alter? A man loves the meat

APPETIZERS

Carpaccio

SERVES 1

- 2 OUNCES BEEF TENDERLOIN
- 1 TABLESPOON POMMEREY MAYONNAISE (1 TABLESPOON MAYONNAISE AND 3/4 TEASPOON POMMEREY MUSTARD)
- 1 TABLESPOON EXTRA VIRGIN OLIVE OIL
- 1 TEASPOON PARMESAN CHEESE, SHAVED
- 1/2 TEASPOON CRACKED BLACK PEPPER
- 1 TOMATO ROSE
- 2 BASIL LEAVES

Trim fat from meat carefully to remove all outside fat. Slice meat as thinly as possible. The meat may be partially frozen to facilitate slicing with a very sharp knife. Place Pommerey mayonnaise on plate in circular pattern. Lay the thinly sliced beef tenderloin over the Pommerey mayonnaise. Drizzle with olive oil. Sprinkle with Parmesan cheese and cracked black pepper. Garnish with tomato rose and fresh basil leaves.

Barlow K. Philipps
Faust's

in his youth that he cannot endure in his age." *Much Ado About Nothing*
WILLIAM SHAKESPEARE

Henry IV, Part I
ALAN ARMSTRONG
COSTUME DESIGNER

APPETIZERS

Sausage Wellington

SERVES 8

1 POUND ITALIAN SAUSAGE LINKS
2 EGGS, WELL BEATEN
2 TABLESPOONS MILK
8 1 EACH PUFF PASTRY SHEET
1/4 CUP PARMESAN CHEESE
MARINARA SAUCE

Suggested wine: Shiraz, Zinfandel or a Montepulciano d'Abruzzo

*Chris Desens
The Country Club
at The Legends*

Bake sausage links halfway through and cool to room temperature. Make a wash of eggs and milk. Roll out puff pastry slightly and brush with egg wash. Sprinkle with Parmesan. Lay sausage in the middle. Roll pastry around sausage and tuck in ends. Place on sheet tray and use egg wash. Sprinkle with Parmesan. Bake in a 400-degree oven for 12 to 15 minutes or until golden brown. Remove from oven. Slice on a diagonal every 1/2 inch. Serve with marinara sauce.

Henry IV, Part I
ALAN ARMSTRONG
COSTUME DESIGNER

INTERMISSION

"If music be the food of love, play on."

Twelfth Night
WILLIAM SHAKESPEARE